KEVIN MILLS

an ounce of
DISCERNMENT

The
OUNCE PROJECT™
Book Seven

ALLUME PRESS

Mills, Kevin

AN OUNCE OF DISCERNMENT
THE OUNCE PROJECT - Book Seven

First trade paperback original edition.

Published by

ALLUME PRESS
Goleta, CA 93117

ISBN 978-0-9765527-3-4

The
OUNCE PROJECT™

www.TheOunceProject.com

*All lyrics are reprinted with permission
from the publishers and authors of From My Whispers
and The Screams of the Feminine.*

*Cover and book design by T. Lacy – design@okdaimyo.com
Calligraphy by Steven Tong – tongtakfong@gmail.com*

This book is dedicated to my mother, Sydanie Mills. A mother in so many different ways to so many different people. Your love, your guidance, and your force are still felt so deeply even though you are no longer with us.
Mom!
I cry!
I scream!
I miss you!

Gratitude

I want to extend deep gratitude to my entire community. You all came together to help bring The Ounce Project into the world. Thank you so much.

To Steven Tong and Simone Tong, you saved me from me. Through your patience, tenderness, and wisdom, you helped to bring deeper meaning to this book through your Calligraphy. Thank you.

To Tim Lacy, my design wizard, your guidance is profound on so many levels. Thank you for taking the time to teach me all you know across so many realms. Thank you.

And to Diana Syvertson, you inspire me as you walk your brave path in this world. Thank you for your steadfast support and always showing up in truth and grace. Thank you.

· About the Author

I am an Advocate for your soul.

For the past 15 years, I have run a private consulting practice focused on advising high net worth individuals. I help people from across the world convene and converse with their soul, the deepest most profound and most eternal part of themselves.

To truly touch meaning in your life, you must first know thyself; you must first know your story, not the way you tell it but the way your soul would tell your story.

After graduating from Harvard Business School, I began walking the path of a high-flying executive. I soon became the CEO of what was at the time one of the largest online learning platforms in Healthcare. Everything, however, changed for me while I was on a trip to Fiji.

I had traveled to Fiji for a date with destiny, but on my way to this very expensive seminar, I experienced my true date with destiny.

Upon my arrival at the Sheraton Hotel in Nadi Fiji, I took an introductory scuba diving course. The very next morning I was sitting on the bow of the dive boat heading out into the ocean. By the end of the first day of diving and listening to the stories of the crew and fellow passengers, I had become fast friends with the captain of the dive boat.

"Kevin," the captain told me at the end of my first day, "come dive tomorrow, but you don't have to sign up at the hotel. Just come and jump on the boat anytime you want, you are now my personal guest on my humble boat." So for the next few days, I did just that.

On the fourth day, I followed my same routine. I climbed onto the boat, and stood next to the captain as he called out his now familiar mantra to all the passengers, "It's another beautiful day in the office!" For over an hour we traveled through the morning sunlight and toward the horizon. As I had done on each of the previous mornings upon arrival at the dive site, I helped the new guests put on their scuba diving gear. However, on this particular morning instead of putting on my tanks, I decided to go snorkeling by myself.

It was such a sweet feeling, floating in the ocean alone with just my thoughts. There were nibbling fish kindly picking away at my skin, it felt like kisses from God. I was in heaven.

Soon, however, I lost track of time; and evidently, I also lost track of the boat for when I surfaced the dive boat had left. The boat, my fellow divers, the crew, and the captain were all gone.

I later learned one of the hotel guests fell so ill the dive was unexpectedly cut short. The captain checked the manifest of passengers and crew, and I was not on either list, so he headed back to shore leaving me in the ocean.

I began screaming. I began screaming at God!

"It is not supposed to be like this," I screamed, "I am not supposed to die here!" The little fish that were once nibbling sweetly at my skin were now torturing me. It felt as if they were all trying to eat me alive.

It was a reckoning for sure... it was a reckoning

with God!

"This cannot be it!" I screamed.

"Stop eating me!" I screamed at the fish.

I was in a total panic screaming, fighting off the nibbling fish and terrified that all the things I knew I was meant to do in the world would now remain undone. I am unsure how long my tirade lasted, but I remember the moment I surrendered and accepted that I was going to die in the middle of the Southern Pacific Ocean; the moment the intense terror within me turned to pure silence. At that moment I could hear everything. I could feel everything. I knew my truth and all I was meant to do with my life, versus the path that had brought me to this very moment.

"I need one more chance," I spoke into the water. "Just one more chance at my life."

Within moments I heard the dive boat heading back in my direction, and I just cried. The captain threw a rope to me and helped me out of the water.

"You left me in the Ocean!" I exclaimed.

"Singa na linga, Singa na linga, I came back for you," was his simple reply. *Singa na linga* means no problem in Fijian.

I heard my soul. To this day, I navigate my world with that deep connection to my truth.

When I came home from Fiji, I sat with a dear friend and told him my story as it had been told to me by my soul in the middle of the South Pacific Ocean. I explained to him how I was going to crash my life and reinvent myself overnight. In response he made me promise that I would change my life little by little, ounce by ounce and The Ounce Project was born.

Over the past decade and a half, The Ounce Project has evolved and blossomed. It is layered, yet simple; profound and deeply elegant; from The Seven Essential Ounces to The Integration Triad; from An Ounce of Discernment to An Ounce of Grief. And it all begins with one question...

What do you need an ounce of?

The Ounce Project has helped thousands of people transform their lives. I am so excited for you and the journey you are about to begin. This daily practice will allow you to listen to your story as told to you by your soul.

Over the next 28 days, we will focus on Discernment and our ability to make better decisions as we navigate our daily lives.

Let us begin...

An Ounce of Discernment

It is said the very first lesson taught by all great masters to their most dedicated students is the art of discernment.

Once mastered, discernment ensures that the student can see through the illusion and experience the truth. Every single day each and every one of us is faced with thousands of decisions. Do I get out of bed? Do I have a salad or tofu for lunch? Do I swipe left or right?

Once mastered, discernment ensures we may read and better understand the signs in our lives. I remember watching a YouTube video, which had gone viral in less than a day, where a man camping in the wilderness was mesmerized at the most impeccable double rainbow decorating the sky. He just kept screaming, "What does this mean? What does this mean?"

How many times per day do we come across signs that we feel require deeper interpretation? What does it mean when that black cat comes from nowhere and runs across our toes as we walk down some random street? What does it mean when the number one or eleven or one hundred and eleven keeps appearing literally everywhere you turn? What does it mean when night after night you keep experiencing the same dream? That dream where you are being chased only to awake exhausted, just as you are about to find out who it is that is chasing you.

Once mastered, discernment ensures you never arrive at those life-jarring crossroads. Do I stay or do

I leave this relationship or this job? Do I become an artist or a doctor? Am I meant to be a writer or an accountant? The truth is there are never really any such crossroads. There is only your truth and your illusions.

For so many of us, we delegate our daily decisions to external forces such as our parents, our friends, our Uber driver or even our favorite bartender. It gets even worse when we delegate to Snapchat, Instagram, Alexa, Siri, or even an article in Cosmo. Alternatively, we fall into distraction or procrastination forgetting our decision not to make a decision is, in fact, a decision — albeit a less than optimal decision. By the way, a less than optimal decision today leads to less than optimal choices tomorrow.

Over time, as we continually delegate our decisions and choices to external forces, our lives begin to lose meaning. It is as if someone else is driving our car and we feel completely out of control.

Do you remember throwing a full-blooded tantrum when you were in kindergarten? Do you remember being in your early teens swearing and raging at your overbearing parents? Do you remember telling someone who claimed they loved you that you feel controlled or invisible in the relationship?

These are examples of each of us fighting or rebelling to take back some aspect of control or decision making from an external influence. Why?

Why do we rebel? Why do we fight for control of our own lives?

I believe within each of us lies our own knowing and personal authority designed to help us better navigate our own lives truly. Ounce by Ounce and day by day this book is designed to deepen your connection to your inner experience so that you may better access your own inner resources and personal wisdom.

Imagine how much easier your life would be without having to clean up the direct messes and indirect consequences associated with those bad decisions that continue to torment you even today.

My goal, my desire is this book helps you make two better decisions today and each day. That's 56 better decisions over the next 28 days, the course of this book.

Take the journey into An Ounce of Discernment and witness your life transform Ounce by Ounce.

I was having a terrible day at work. My boss had pushed me to the edge, and I was ready to punch him. At that moment I remembered your question, and I asked myself, "What do I need an ounce of?" The response came back, "An Ounce of Self Control." I gave myself that Ounce of Self Control and the moment passed and everything was OK. At least for now.

Told to the Author by A. M.

What is The Ounce Project?

A divinely inspired, moment-to-moment transformational practice designed to reconnect each of us to our original purpose on this planet.

What do you need an ounce of?

By asking one simple question, we can connect our inner world to our outer experience and transform our lives, Ounce by Ounce. By asking ourselves this question we instantly access a place inside of us that is longing to be heard. And because we are only asking for an ounce, we are compelled to give ourselves An Ounce of Serenity or An Ounce of Self Control or An Ounce of Grief, Anger or Bliss.

The more we ask the question and the more we listen to our own response and the more we give ourselves what we need — Ounce by Ounce — we build an intricate trust between our inner world and our outer experience, and I promise you will begin to navigate your life in an entirely new and profound manner.

What do you need an ounce of?

Write it down right now! Give yourself an ounce of whatever it is that you need, right now!

Remember we live our lives moment-to-moment, and in any given moment our lives may shift or tilt or take a very unexpected turn in either a positive or negative way. I invite you to begin your practice today. So...

What do you need an ounce of?

How to Use This Book

Take a journey for 28 days.

Start your morning by reading and using your ounce for the day. Meditate on the calligraphy. It will help ground you into the meaning of each word. Witness how that ounce helps you to navigate your world.

Please write every day. Write in your journal or this book. Your written words will also help to ground and integrate your experience.

When you reach the end of this book, please feel free to repeat this process, and rest assured that everything will feel very different the second or third time through.

Alternatively please give yourself An Ounce of Discernment each day for 28 days and witness how deeply your life will change, shift and evolve.

Please remember that at any point during this process feel free to simply open the book to whatever page seems to be calling to you.

Let us begin. Ask yourself right now:

What do you need an ounce of?

Write here . . .

This space is provided at the end of each chapter as an invitation for you to begin your journal entry for the day. In the following pages I have included journal entries from other readers on their 28-day journey. Please feel free to post photos of your journal entries.

#Theounceproject

Messages from Their Journeys for You . . .

Write here . . .

I was in a class today that was very challenging to keep up with. I love classes like this, especially from this teacher, but I often miss words, phrases, or lessons due to zoning out. An Ounce of Presence was written on my wrist in thin Sharpie. Several times I looked down on it and remembered my commitment to Presence today.
I interpreted this Ounce of Presence in a small way. Just staying focused and present for the next few moments, the next few words. Like in meditation, it was a constant re-start tool for when my mind wandered. I definitely felt I had a strong, helpful tool at my disposal to continue focusing in class. :-)

TB

The
OUNCE PROJECT

Write here . . .

Just now I was muttering about wishing for an ounce of respect or appreciation as I was cleaning up toys and clutter. I love that I received an ounce of Trust instead. I need to trust that my husband and my kids love, respect and appreciate me and my hard work. As I get ready to go out dancing all night long, I also want to start with an ounce of Trust for the DJs – that they will take us on a journey that was meant to be.

AH

The
OUNCE PROJECT

Write here . . .

I am certain
I am on the right path
I am grounded
I have released
I have refined
I am certain
I am not alone
I am guided, protected and the steps are laid
before me
I am certain I have found my strength
I am connected
I am ready
I trust,
I know truth
. . . let's continue.

NB

Write here . . .

Today I was walking to work after a
long phone call with my Mom, who I've
previously mentioned is dealing with a sever
bout of cancer. I was feeling very nervous
and afraid for her, for me, for my whole
family. I used the Ounce of Trust, and it gave
me just enough feeling that I could trust in
Life, in God, in the grand scheme of things,
and I really settled down. It was a very useful
Ounce today.

TB

The
OUNCE PROJECT

Write here . . .

I am Up earlier today and getting x-rays on
my spine for pain. I appreciate the familiarity
of this meditation and the buzz my body
feels at the end, even if my mind wandered
a bit.

WW

Chapter One

Introductory Ounces

Day One – Day Seven

Remember this process is all about learning how to listen to your true voice that resides within you.

*Remember this is your journey, not mine.
Even though this book is here as a guide,
you are the only one who can take this journey.*

*Remember, chapter one is simply an introduction.
Play, have fun, and please remember you do not
get any extra points for making things harder than
they are or harder than they really need to be.*

We are playing ounce by ounce.

Day 1

吐
故
納
新

an ounce of . . .

Breath

INHALE

EXHALE

You must breathe, especially at the times
when you least feel like breathing.

What does an ounce of breath mean to you?

Deeper!

Deeper!

When I learned how to breathe, I found I had
more capacity to sing and more capacity for life.

Do you know how to breathe so that
you may increase your capacity for life?

Write here . . .

Day 2

無
庸
置
疑

an ounce of . . .

Certainty

"Daddy, I believe singing is your third favorite thing in the entire world." I was lying with my four-year-old son in my arms singing him a lullaby. Out of pure curiosity I asked him the most obvious question.

"So what is my second favorite thing in the entire world?"

"Soccer," he responded, without hesitation and yet half asleep. His sweet voice played kindly in my ear. I smiled and nodded and finished my questioning.

"So baby," I whispered very gently. He was almost asleep now, "what is my most favorite thing in the entire world?" And with his last breath as he fell into his dreams for the night he whispered back to me, "Why me, of course."

I wish I'd had my son's certainty
when I was his age, in fact, I wish
I had his certainty in my world right now!

What in your life are you certain of?

If you had an Ounce of Certainty at this moment,
what would you permit yourself to do?

Write here . . .

Day 3

傾囊相助

an ounce of . . .

Everything

A Wiseman once told me, "When you are walking through hell, keep walking," and I did. I walked all night with a head filled with questions and distractions and with my eyes in search of signs from God that he had answered my prayer. The streets of the city were cold, bare and at times scary, but I kept walking.

I found myself at the door of a small coffee shop seeking refuge from the brisk morning air. I had walked all night with my desire for confirmation of some sort. The sun was beginning to climb into the morning sky. After buying my coffee, I took my place at a table hidden in a corner. In the opposite corner of the coffee shop, there was a homeless woman who was cursing at a man in a wheelchair.

"You no-legged, good for nothing, son-of-a-bitch," she yelled at the cripple. The man in the wheelchair cursed back but as well as having no legs he also had no teeth, so I can't swear to what he called her in return. Then out of nowhere, she looked at me, and without invitation, she walked over to my table. Her harsh tone reached out to me, licking me with a certain amount of softness.

"You're new here," she told me, "I will show you where to sleep so no one will bother you." She continued to teach me, "Don't buy coffee here, just get a cup and there is a hotel around the corner where you can sneak in and get free coffee, but don't tell anyone else." I listened as she taught me her ways of survival. She believed that I was homeless.

For a moment I sank into myself, embarrassed, scared and paralyzed with no idea of what to say to this woman, what to say to myself. Out of my blind spot, I heard a voice in my head. It whispered so softly I almost missed it, "do you see God in her eyes?" So Bizarre! I heard the voice as clear as day. I followed the instructions, and I looked into her eyes. The voice in my head continued, "do you see God in your eyes?" Then this homeless woman who now sat opposite me reached her hand down into her panties, pulled out a dollar bill and offered it to me. I hesitated since I did not want to take money from a homeless woman and I was not entirely sure what else she had stored in her panties.

"Please take it," she spoke to me in the sweetest of voices, "please take it; it is all I have, but you need it more than I do; I can go make more."

I hesitated. So many emotions ran through me at that moment. Before I could come to a clear decision about whether accepting the woman's gift was a sign or the answer to my prayer, I took the dollar bill and held it in my hand. It felt alive. Her words rang and rattled through my bones, "It is all I have, but don't worry I can make more." I took her gift and in the next moment she turned to her legless friend and began cursing once more.

I was left sitting with my dollar bill.

I was sitting with everything.

What would An Ounce of Everything look like to you?

What would you do in the world
if you had An Ounce of Everything?

Write here . . .

Day 4

山盟海誓

an ounce of . . .

Commitment

I was in Jamaica watching local television just before the 2015 Pan Am Regatta. For the first time in history, Jamaica was entering a team into this major rowing event. They had been practicing for months, and everything was going well. The entire country was very proud of this new accomplishment. The reporter from the local news station asked one of the rowers after one of their final practices before heading off to the competition, "It is so close to the Regatta, when are you going to learn how to swim?"

The Rower responded, "Why do I need to learn how to swim? I am in the boat!"

Commitment, Ounce by Ounce!

Are you in the boat?
Your boat, your life as you have dreamt it?

Or do you have multiple backup plans
just in case you fall into the water?

What does An Ounce of Commitment
mean to you at this moment?

How committed are you to_____?
(Please fill in the blank.)

Write here . . .

The
OUNCE PROJECT

Day 5

天
荒
地
荒

an ounce of . . .

Love

It is said that Eskimos have more than 50 words to describe snow. I believe that we need at least as many words to describe Love.

When you ask for Love, what Love are you asking for?

When you give love, what kind of love do you give?

*What would An Ounce of Love feel like
to you right now at this moment?*

Write here . . .

Day 6

心曠神怡

an ounce of . . .
Bliss

△

I came here explicitly to cleanse
Clear away my muck
Realign my lens
I dove deep within on my quest
I swore I'd toil and strive
There would be no rest
But then I met you
And you
And you
And you
And you, shifted my worldview with conversations
about that and about this
And about joy and about bliss
With questions such as what is love?
And how do I find my guidance from above?
So I sat with healers and mystics
I drank tea and biscuits
But it was in the pour
In the rain, when God began to explain
So may I take a moment right now.
Please accept my bow
I honor completely who you are and the journey you
have chosen thus far
So please, would you take a moment
And take a look into the eyes of another

Maybe your brother?
Your sister?
Maybe the eyes of your lover?
I promise, in those eyes rests the answer to your quest
Rests
The human divine's best
Rests
The milk from a mother's breast
Rests
all that you need
feed, I plead
This moment do not waste
Savor the taste
Nourish your soul
Be whole
Be whole
May I take a moment right now?
Please, accept my bow
I honor how brave you are and the journey you have
chosen thus far
As for me, soon I will leave this place
With that taste
Until it is my turn
To return
To this place
Which in turn
Will help me to learn
About that
And about this
And about joy
And about bliss

What is bliss to you?

How will you give yourself An Ounce of Bliss?

Please be as creative as your imagination will allow!

Write here . . .

The
OUNCE PROJECT

Day 7

赤

子

之

心

an ounce of . . .

Soul

What do you need an ounce of?

*There is a place deep within each of us
from which our most profound knowings emanate.*

*If you are willing to ask the question and listen,
your soul will whisper back to you.*

*That is the journey, to connect to our deepest selves
and navigate our world in pure alignment.*

So...

What do you need an ounce of?

Write here . . .

Messages from Their Journeys for You . . .

Write here . . .

Today, I want to let go of self-doubt and shame. Today, I will let go of feeling not good enough. I instead trade my shame for the excitement that my dad had a big breakthrough moment concerning his health. Six months ago, I was dreaming for the breakthrough I had today with him and his ability to heal. I am with the right people, at the right time, and on the right path. I let go of beating myself up. Instead, I'd like to celebrate how far I've come. I am doing it.

MJ

The
OUNCE PROJECT

Write here . . .

Today I decided to do things a little different at work, so instead of my usually strict headmistress style my approach was a little less harsh and let up on the students. I laughed and listened more; it was a good day.

VM

The
OUNCE PROJECT

Write here . . .

When I consider an Ounce of Refinement, the most immediate answer is to refine my expectations in the short term concerning work. I'm working in a few creative fields at once, and they sort of overlap at points. As of 2018, the fields I work in are all enhanced through an online presence. While I experiment and try my hand, I'm continually exposed to "experts" giving me both complimentary and contrasting advice. It's making my head spin. When I use an Ounce of Refinement, I remember that I do not need to take everyone's advice. That I can play the game making sure I would actually like what I'm putting out. And my expectations that I should be able to do it all right now are refined to moving through one manageable project at a time.

TB

The
OUNCE PROJECT™

Write here . . .

Love is my word that I need to refine. I can't love someone and expect their love to be just as strong as my love for them. I have to choose to whom to give my love and only choose those that want the love that I'm giving. I'm certain the only true love that I will ever know is from the love of me. I'm re-learning how to love me again and not have any expectations of love from others.

VM

Write here . . .

My blind spot to love was being able to face my emotion, feel it all the way through and balance the light mystery and dark mystery flow.

TB

.

The
OUNCE PROJECT

Chapter Two

Seven Essential Ounces

Day Eight – Day Fourteen

*Remember, if you can master these seven
essential ounces your ability to make exquisite
conscious decisions will be greatly enhanced…*

But there is more…

*Remember, as you deepen your relationship
with the mystery, the unknown that is your soul,
your ability to navigate your outer-world
becomes so much easier…*

And there is even more…

*Remember, if you can master these seven
essential ounces you will become a great lover…*

*YOU ARE WELCOME!
The details are in my next book.*

Day 8

競
業

an ounce of . . .

Grounding

Finding my tree in the middle of a city was almost an impossible task. I would approach a tree and ask if I may touch its skin. I was surprised at how many trees screamed *NO!* But this is the city after all. Many trees had been transplanted into a foreign place, into an unnatural place, with their roots fighting to keep a grip.

When I finally found my tree, she welcomed me, embraced me. It is now the place where I go so that I may find my way back to myself. She shares her wisdom, her love, her grief and hundreds of years of being part of this planet called earth.

How do you ground?

*How do you calm your system down
once you're triggered?*

*Does it always work the way
you want it to work for you?*

And what do you do when it does not work for you?

*We all need a way back to ourselves,
what is your path back to yourself?*

Write here . . .

Day 9

專心致志

an ounce of . . .

Presence

I was sitting with the Witch in the Woods. I had heard all of these stories about her and her ability to clear your path of anything that may be standing in your way, almost like sitting with Ganesh. Except this was the Witch in the Woods. The man who first told me about this particular witch said, "You have to call her and leave her a message, but you should know she will only call you back if she feels the need. Sometimes," he continued, "some people call her but never ever hear from her."

I followed my instructions very carefully and left her a message, and I waited. I waited and the days turned into weeks, and I waited. One grey cloudy morning my phone rang and to my surprise it was her calling me. As I said hello, I felt tingles run up and down my spine.

"Who are you?" she asked. I explained everything and she told me she could see me that day and only that day. She gave me directions and within an hour I was on my way into the woods to find the Witch.

When I arrived, I was very deep in the woods and I walked cautiously up to her door. I knocked and waited.

When she answered her door, she smiled at me, and at least at first she did not look or feel very witch-like.

She told me, "We are going to chat for ten minutes, and then I am going to lay you on the table and put you in a light trance…"

So I started talking, and we talked and talked. About two hours into our conversation, she stopped very abruptly, "Did you see that?" she asked. She waited only a moment before repeating her question, only this time with a lot more force, "Did you see that?" Without waiting for a response, she just screamed, "You just arrived. It took almost two hours for all of you to arrive in this moment. YOU ARE HERE NOW!"

She paused and took a very deep breath. I felt complete as if all fragments of Humpy Dumpty's pieces were suddenly put back together.

"We are done," she stated with pure clarity, "I should not really charge you for this session," she said, "…but I am going to charge you for wasting my time. Just show up next time."

What does An Ounce of Presence mean to you?

What is your go-to mode of distraction?

*How do you ensure that you are
present in each moment?*

Write here . . .

Day 10

洗耳恭聽

an ounce of . . .

Listening

When a woman in a particular African tribe knows she is pregnant, she goes into the wilderness with a few friends to pray and meditate together until they hear the song of the unborn child. They recognize that every soul has its unique vibration that expresses its flavor and purpose. When the women attune to the song, they sing it out loud. Then they return to the tribe and teach it to everyone else.

When the child is born, the community gathers and sings the child's song to him or her. Later, when the child enters education, the village gathers and chants the child's song. When the child passes through the initiation to adulthood, the people again come together and sing. At the time of marriage, the person hears his or her song. Finally, when the soul is about to pass from this world, the family and friends gather at the person's bed, just as they did at their birth, and they sing the person to the next life.

In the African tribe, there is one other occasion upon which the villagers sing to the child. If at any time during his or her life, the person commits a crime or aberrant social act, the individual is called to the center of the village, and the people in the community form a circle around them. Then they sing their song to them. The tribe recognizes that the correction for antisocial behavior is not punishment; it is love and the remembrance of identity. When you understand your song, you have no desire or need to do anything that would hurt another.

A friend is someone who knows your song and sings it to you when you have forgotten it.

Those who love you are not fooled by mistakes you have made or dark images you hold about yourself. They remember your beauty when you feel ugly; your wholeness when you feel broken; your innocence when you feel guilty; and your purpose when you feel confused.

You may not have grown up in an African tribe that sings your song to you at crucial life transitions, but life is always reminding you when you are in tune with yourself and when you are not.

When you feel good, what you are doing matches your song, and when you feel awful, it doesn't. In the end, we shall all recognize our song and sing it well.

You may feel a little wobbly sometimes, but so have all the great singers. Just keep singing, and you'll find your way home.

Alan Cohen

An ounce of listening, what does that mean to you?

How does that feel in your body?

*If you listen closely enough, you may
be able to hear the beat of the universe,
the rhythm of the earth...inside you,
like hearing the ocean in a seashell...*

What do you hear inside you?

Write here . . .

Day 11

格守京渝

an ounce of . . .

Trust

In a brilliant book by Joellen Koerner called *Mother Heal My Self* she documents how as the Head Nurse of one of the largest hospital systems in the Midwest, helplessly watching her daughter die during childbirth. At her darkest moment in the parking lot of that hospital, a Native American Shaman approached and asked to see her daughter. The medical doctors had given up all hope, as they could not understand how or why Joellen's daughter was dying.

The Shaman asked her daughter a simple question, "Tell me about the stories you have heard about dying during childbirth?" Her daughter began sharing her stories. She told the Shaman of all the stories she had overheard as a child. The stories of her aunt and great-aunt, generations of women in their family dying during childbirth. Joellen's daughter believed this was hereditary and she was destined to succumb and sacrifice her life during childbirth.

The Shaman listened through all the screams that rang throughout the room until there were no more stories. He said a prayer and reminded Joellen's daughter that she had a choice, even in this life and death situation she still had a choice.

I am grateful to share that I was told this story by Joellen Koerner well before there was a book, and the layers of trust she set in motion at that moment has transformed many lives including my own.

The Shaman said his prayer, Joellen's daughter made her choice and gave birth to a beautiful child. They both lived.

Whom do you trust?

Whom do you not trust and why?

What does an ounce of trust mean to you?

*What family stories have been passed down to you,
good stories or challenging stories?*

Write here . . .

Day 12

明月

察

秋

亳

an ounce of . . .

Discernment

I was having a terrible day at work. My boss had pushed me to the edge, and I was ready to punch him. At that moment I remembered your question, and I asked myself, "What do I need an ounce of?" The response came back, "An Ounce of Self Control." I gave myself that Ounce of Self Control and the moment passed and everything was OK. At least for now.

A. M.

*Moments can tilt our lives,
and they can tilt our lives forever.*

*Do I stay in that relationship even
though I know it is really toxic for me?*

*Do I stay in the job that is draining every ounce
of energy from my body every day of the week?*

*What is the choice you know
you need to make at this moment?*

*What is the consequence of
not deciding at this moment?*

*Tell me about a moment when a decision
that you made tilted your life
in a completely different direction?
(It could be positive or negative.)*

Write here . . .

Day 13

千金一諾

an ounce of . . .

Permission

From an astrological perspective, it takes the planet Saturn 28 years to return to the exact place where it sat in the sky when we were born. During that first 28 years all of our decisions are influenced and driven by external forces, such as family, culture, religion, rules and expectations imposed by others like teachers, friends, and even our famous icons or personal heroes.

Typically, at the age of somewhere around 26 years for women and 30 for men, we hit a crisis when we realize all of our decisions have been externally driven. At this point our crisis is meant to drive us to realign our lives and begin living from a place that is driven from within, driven by our purpose. Unfortunately, however, during this crisis many of us do the opposite and double down, creating lives burdened by more external obligations, such as debt, houses, children.

In the scientific realm, Saturn's return is referred to as the threshold of maturity. Neuroscientists believe that the brain is not fully developed: the thinning of grey matter and the thickening of white matter continues until the age of 30. There is also a phenomenon known as the 27 Club, which is the age that many famous artists such as Janis Joplin, Jimi Hendrix, Amy Winehouse, Kurt Cobain, and Jim Morrison died or committed suicide. From an astrological perspective, it is the point when an artist, even a rebel artist, realizes that their work has all been driven from the outside.

Over the past ten years or so the external influences have been greatly exacerbated by the introduction of social media and technological "advances." According to estimations, the average person sees between 4,000 and 10,000 ads per day, depending on the environment (NYC vs. Yosemite) and social media use. Additionally, we have become fully dependent upon our technology. In 2016, a Canadian women drove her car directly into the Georgian Lake because she followed her GPS. Even though her own eyes told her she was approaching a lake, she continued following the instructions from her GPS.

What would An Ounce of Permission
feel like for you in this very moment...
Just an ounce, just a little bit?

What would be possible for you
if you gave yourself An Ounce of Permission?

Write here . . .

Day 14

融
會
貫
通

an ounce of . . .

Integration

I remember listening to a story featured on RadioLab about the transition of a caterpillar into a butterfly. I was blown away to discover caterpillars have wings. They have wings! Caterpillars crawl around on the ground and yet they have the capability of flying. That fact made me think about human DNA. There's so much of our DNA that scientists do not yet understand? Why it is there? Maybe that dark matter, or junk, was intentionally built into our DNA and in it, we have stored our wings. What if we only need to cocoon and evolve, like the caterpillar and the butterfly, for us to discover our built-in ability to fly?

The radio show also examined the process of transformation, tracking what happened inside the chrysalis after the caterpillar surrenders its life and takes on a new appearance as a pod. They found inside the chrysalis everything first turns to goo. Then, like the most complicated jigsaw puzzle ever created, all of the goo reforms itself into a fully functioning, unique and beautiful butterfly. It's as if all the parts of the butterfly already existed within the insect we once knew as a caterpillar, and then with nothing added except death and rebirth — WALLAH — it becomes an entirely new version of itself, the butterfly.

I imagine tiny little workers inside the chrysalis

slaving away night and day, screaming at each other, "Where does this go? Do we need this part in this model?" Those tiny little butterfly workers innovate and craft a unique, one-of-a-kind, custom-built creature of pure perfection and beauty. Like a snowflake, so many have come before but not like this, not like this!

On the journey from goo, when do those tiny little workers inside of the chrysalis say, "Enough is enough?" How do they know when they have traveled deep enough, far enough, and melted enough into goo — pure goo — so that the rebuilding process may begin?

*If we can take random bytes of information and turn
it into knowledge and then walk our world with our
knowledge until it becomes our experience.*

*If we can take our experience and release that which
was never really relevant then we end up at wisdom.*

*We become the wisdom keepers for
the generations to come after us.*

Maybe this is the why integration is so important?

What does it mean for you to integrate?

How do you integrate?

Write here . . .

How The Seven Essential Ounces Align

An Ounce of Grounding – First we ground and come home to ourselves and who we truly are…

An Ounce of Presence – This brings us into the present moment, breaking us out of whatever situation, trigger or loop has currently ensnared us.

An Ounce of Listening – We listen, and we hear the small whisper from within that helps connect our inner world to our external experience.

An Ounce of Trust – The more we listen, the more we trust our inner source.

An Ounce of Discernment – We must master the art of discernment, choosing at this moment which is free of expectation of self or self-rigidity. Discernment, to choose in the moment for the moment.

An Ounce of Permission – Granting conscious permission to oneself, maybe one of the hardest things for us humans to do.

An Ounce of Integration – Once we ask the question and come home to self, we come into the moment and begin to listen and deepen our trust of self. Then we choose and ignite that choice with our permission. Every time we flow through this moment-to-moment practice we are changed. Our connection to our true self is elevated. So we integrate and begin the flow again from this new place.

Messages from Their Journeys for You . . .

Write here . . .

I just went through the Essential 7 Ounces and felt a clearer understanding of how they can work together in my life. And it helped me regain footing in the way of life I've been living. I have recently been successfully noticing where I am blocked in my life, things that "trigger" me, or situations that elicit a habited response. As I understand it, following these habited responses leads to a less adventurous, less fulfilled life. After integrating the 7 Essentials, in the moment of asking for Manifestation, it came to me that instead of wanting the perfect job, or perfect person to grow my acting or writing career, I could ask to continue manifesting things that challenge me to grow myself. Because then I can continue breaking down bad habits and boldly stepping towards responsibility and growth, which is truthfully more exciting.

TB

The
OUNCE PROJECT

Write here . . .

An ounce of Grounding. Interesting that today I did a meditation before responding to emails, before the to-do list, before even getting changed. It was by accident because I WAS checking emails and "The Ounce Project" in my inbox caught my eye. Interesting that today I meditated for over 11 minutes when I normally struggle to cram it into my 7-min morning commute while driving or while doing make-up in the car of the parking lot of my office. During the meditation, I felt a flood of emotion and memories. I remembered a tarot card reading from 15 years ago where I pulled a card of someone driving a chariot without reigns. I've often felt that — that I have an abundance of energy, but I'm not directing it. I understand that Grounding is critical for me to take the reigns.

AN

The
OUNCE PROJECT

Write here . . .

I give myself permission To love
To cry
To heal
To hurt
To trust
To move forward
To ask
To be patient
To receive
To go back
To listen And to let go
I give myself permission to walk in my truth.
To be me

NB

The
OUNCE PROJECT™

Write here . . .

I was able to give myself permission to be me, and in doing so gave permission for others to make their own choices.

TB

Write here . . .

trust
or
not to trust
that is the question . . . .
option 1 trust . . . .
I can breathe
Option 2
not to trust
I am not breathing . . . .

I choose option 1

VS

The
OUNCE PROJECT

Chapter Three

Discernment Ounces

Day Fifteen – Day Twenty-Five

*Remember, during the next eleven days
your journey into the art of conscious
decision making, Discernment truly begins.*

*Ounce-by-Ounce we will explore and
clear the aspects of your being that distort
or interrupt your ability to make clear,
honest decisions for yourself.*

*Remember, your old stories and beliefs,
your cultural or family forces,
or even a lack of chocolate may impede
your ability to be present in this moment
to hear your truth and have the courage
to act in alignment with that truth.*

*Remember, an ounce per day is more than enough.
And an ounce per day grows on itself
not incrementally, but exponentially.*

Let's Play…

Day 15

Story

明月察秋毫

an ounce of . . .

Discernment

Once upon a time, I started telling my stories. And once I started, they kept coming. I never realized how many stories I had. They seemed random. They were random. They stemmed from many different aspects of my life.

As I told them, I wasn't sure if the facts were straight, but I told them from feeling. I told them from a very deep place, a very connected place, a place that needed to be released. I told them from my anger, from my hurt, from my love, from mystery, from dreams. I told them, and they kept coming.

Eventually, I had enough stories; I believe they numbered about ten. My stories seemed to be a random set of ramblings, a disjointed mirage, a murky, muddy mess of emotions, feelings, and thoughts. My stories were raw, honest, and at times I could not take the honesty for another second. I had to hide in my distraction, any distraction. There were just some places I did not want to go. I flat out refused to go.

After playing, breathing, coming and going, I finally got to some of those places but, honestly, there are places I am yet to visit. And I may never visit, and that's okay with me.

Once upon a time, I started telling my stories. And once I told them I had to share them. Now, that's a scary thought. I felt that if I shared these most intimate pieces of me, I would be rejected, ostracized, abandoned on a roadside. So I decided to find those I trusted.

When I asked myself whom do I trust, I came up with some strange answers — certainly not the usual or expected suspects. I found those who saw me whole, those who knew my eyes, and I knew theirs.

At first there were only a few who fit the description, so I shared my stories with them. They found themes in my stories, threads that I could not see. They asked why. They told me of places where I was not honest. They requested more from me. They taught me my mistakes make magic.

They promised to stand with me as I navigated my uncharted waters. They told me of my blind spots, and then I was blind no more: Layers and layers, shedding of layers. Those I trusted became my inner community. They became my tribe.

Once upon a time, I started telling my stories. And once I told them I had to share them. And once I shared them, I let them go, and I created so much space in my body, space for new experiences, space for expanding old stories into new adventures, space for love, space for life, space for this moment.

Once upon a time, I started telling my stories. And once I told them I had to share them. And once I shared them I let them go. Once I let them go, I began writing new stories.

Stories not bound by my past threads.

Stories of me just being me.

Stories of adventures, stories that I once knew very well but at some point had given up on, and now those stories are here again.

I found myself dreaming all over again, making wishes in wells, expecting miracles, experiencing magic in simple moments, loving life, and simply loving.

Once upon a time I started telling my stories, and

once I told them I had to share them, and once I shared them, I let them go, and once I let them go, I began writing new stories.

But here is the amazing thing: I am no longer writing new stories; I am now living them. Loving them.

What a beautiful notion.

What are your stories?

Do they bind you to your past
or do they set you free?

Whom do you trust enough to share
your most intimate stories with?

Which stories are you willing to let go?

Which stories do you intend to keep?

Why?

Write here . . .

Day 16

Replaying The Movie In Your Life

明
察
秋
毫

an ounce of . . .

Discernment

My niece loves *Frozen*. Of course, I am referring to the Disney movie. She loves the movie so much that when her younger sister was born, she persuaded her mother to name her new sibling Elsa. When I go to visit her, I am Uncle Olaf. Please don't ask me to explain since I have never seen the movie, but apparently, I remind her of a snowman.

In a recent session, a client shared with me that her favorite childhood Disney movie was *Beauty and The Beast*. It became clear that from an unconscious place she had been recreating situations in her life that mirrored the plot and drama from her favorite movie. The most interesting and yet most confusing aspect of her situation was, even though she was a beautiful woman in her twenties, she identified herself with the beast in the movie. Once we arrived at this point of clarity, her life began to make so much sense and then she was free to make new decisions for herself beyond the plot of Disney's *Beauty and The Beast*.

Many people are trapped or keep
recreating their favorite movie and so:

What is your favorite Disney movie?

You must have seen it at least ten times,
and if not a Disney movie, what was
your favorite movie as a child?

Which character reminds you most of yourself?

How have you been recreating your life
around the plot of this movie?

Who are the other characters in your life that are
playing a role directly from your favorite movie?

Write here . . .

Day 17

Mistakes Make Magic

明
察
秋
毫

an ounce of . . .

Discernment

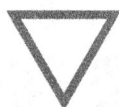

A legendary Jazz artist once stated there are no mistakes, no wrong notes in Jazz... everything is always about what you do with the next note...

*For sure sometimes my life feels like a totally
improvised and unruly Jazz jam session,
with random players riffing off others. When it
all flows, we create totally unexpected melodies
that begin with a finger strumming a string;
expand to catch fire in my soul until the sound
echoes back into the world, and I hear myself
scream, "What the hell was that?"*

*What are the mistakes you have made,
that ultimately turned into moments of magic?*

*Remember it is your next decision
that matters the most.*

*Remember it is your next decision that
you have the most control over...*

What is your next conscious decision?

Write here . . .

Day 18

Know Thy Source

明月

察秋

毫

an ounce of . . .

Discernment

About nine months ago I walked into a room, and there was a movie playing. I don't know the name of the movie, but in this scene that I happened upon, one man was speaking wisely to another. He said, "Imagine you're standing in a busy street here on Earth. You have your perspective of what is happening around you, the people, the traffic, and the noise. Now imagine there's a man twenty floors up looking down at the same busy street. He has a different perspective. The man that is twenty floors up is not God. He just has a different perspective. If that man were to call down to you as you stood on that busy street and warn you of an impending accident or a congested street up ahead, that does not make him God. He just has a different perspective."

After watching that scene, I immediately left the room. As I walked out of the room, there was one additional insight that came to me. If the man from twenty floors above screams down to you as you stand in the busy street, what you may hear may be very different from what he originally said. *Know thy source.*

With the new energy present on Earth, it is most critical that we develop a relationship with our source. Whatever your source may be. Not a cursory relationship but rather a deep, rich, tested, proven relationship. Almost like a sincere lover. Know thy source. What do you ask your source for? Do you ask for guidance? Do you ask for reassurance? For love? Do you ask your source to answer your prayers? Finding a trusted source both in the physical and beyond is by no means an easy journey. But it is an essential journey, and from my experience, the journey begins with knowing thyself and grounding deeply into the truth of who you really are.

What or who is your source:
God, the Universe, Google, Oprah?

What is your relationship with your source
and how did you develop this relationship?

Please list the people whom you trust
to help you make important decisions?

What perspective do they bring
to your decision making?

Write here . . .

Day 19

Finding Serenity

明月
察秋
毫

an ounce of . . .

Discernment

God grant me the Serenity to accept the things
I cannot change,

The courage to change the things I can,

And wisdom to know the difference.

The Serenity Prayer

*One of the hardest aspects of conscious
decision making is truly knowing when to let go,
truly accepting things the way they are
and your inability to change them.*

*Or what may be more accurate:
you may not be able to change them right now.*

What does An Ounce of Serenity feel like to you?

Where do you feel it in your body?

How do you rest?

How do you find your center?

Write here . . .

The
OUNCE PROJECT™

Day 20

The Power of Your Grief

明
月
察
秋
毫

an ounce of . . .

Discernment

Our lives are defined by our grief!

From the eight year old who's first love refused his valentine or even worse refused to hold his hand; to my son who at five years old cried for days after watching Mufasa die the first time he watched The Lion King; or the day our beloved pet wandered off and for some reason decided not to return home.

Our lives are defined by our grief!

It was three hours before my mother's funeral, and I was a basket case. I had been crying all night long. I was scheduled to give three speeches at the funeral, and I had not yet put one word to paper.

I had always seen grief as a sign of weakness. I was so afraid of my grief, so afraid that my grief would totally consume me, so afraid that once I let my grief in I would start crying and simply would never stop.

My mother had been my anchor on the planet and all of a sudden she was gone. I was attempting to be strong for my father and my brothers and sisters but as her funeral approached by resolve was waning.

When my Irish twin passed away three years earlier, I had dealt with my grief from his loss by not allowing my grief to touch me in any way what so ever. When my mother passed away, all the grief that I had been avoiding at all cost, came cascading down through my being like an avalanche of virgin snow set free from a mountaintop.

Our lives are defined by our struggle with our grief, and yet we are never taught about our grief, what it is or how to deal with it.

Out of the blue, I asked myself the question that I had taught all my clients over the past ten years.

"What do you need an ounce of?" I asked myself from a place of pure desperation. I immediately I heard from deep within "An Ounce of Grief!" It seemed such a strange response given I was totally consumed by grief at that moment. But in an inexplicable way that additional ounce of grief calmed me down. At that moment, it became my choice to step into my grief just an ounce at a time and then there was space for me inside my grief. I sat on my bed and wrote my speeches.

Our lives are defined by our grief, an ounce at a time.

I gave myself an ounce of grief every day for the next 90 days. At first I tried to control my date with my grief, but I was never in control. Over time, however, my grief began to trust me and I began to trust it. It was as if my grief knew I would come back each day and so after an ounce of grief I would be released. There were days when I went deep, really deep. A moment came in which my grief finally revealed — and released — all the pain and anguish I had stored in my body.

Our lives are defined and beautified and sweetly enhanced by our grief if we can only get to know it, be gentle with it and ourselves. Our grief will teach us and will make us cry and feel, and our grief will be there for us if we will allow it… Ounce by Ounce.

My grief now walks with me like an intimate lover.

Grief is one of those emotions that can distort your ability to clearly discern. Until you gain a better understanding of your grief, your decisions may not be as conscious as we would like them to be.

Grief, fear, abandonment, anger, anxiety, and regret are just a few examples of the emotions that can torment us, and yet there are ways to transform those feelings so that they may act as your guide as you navigate your world.

What is the emotion that most distorts your experience and ability to make conscious decisions?

What is the story that underlies that emotion?

When you are ready, and only when you are ready, please give yourself an ounce of that emotion every day for the next week.

If you need to bookmark this page, please do, but I need you to promise that you will try this exercise.

Write here . . .

Day 21

Refine, Refine, Refine

明察秋毫

an ounce of . . .

Discernment

Throughout my personal journey into self-discovery, I have tried numerous times to remove core beliefs that were no longer relevant. One such example was my belief that, "Everyone was in my life for a reason…" For years I attempted to remove this belief, but it was core to who I had become on the planet. Thus, no matter how hard I tried, that belief and all of it's consequences would soon return. For me, however, it was not until I realized I had to refine and not remove my belief that everything changed. It was almost like upgrading my software. My new belief is, "Everyone is in my life for a reason including telling them to go take a long walk off a short plank… if necessary." My new belief has opened up more space for me so I may invest more of my time and energy with the souls I truly love.

What belief do you hold that you would like to refine?

How would you like to refine that belief?

What does it sound like or feel like?

Write here . . .

Day 22

Pure Curiosity

明察秋毫

an ounce of...

Discernment

Many years ago I was teaching at a well-renowned small liberal arts college. Even though I was teaching an Entrepreneurial Management course, I wanted my students to become more curious about their world around them. More curious about those things or people we take for granted around us. For a homework assignment, I asked my class to find another student whom they did not know and ask that person to tell them a story. Their assignment was simple:

Listen to the stories of another;

Report two things back to class:
1) What did they learn about the other person from their stories?
2) And more importantly, what did they learn about themselves?

In the following class Daniel told his story, saying: *After the last class I walked back to my dorm, and as I entered my building, a student whom I had seen before but had never spoken to was leaving. I stopped her and said I have this crazy professor and we have to find someone and listen to his or her stories. At first she told me she didn't have any stories, but I could tell there was something wrong so I insisted. She began telling me her stories and we sat for hours and I just listened. As we were leaving, she told me she was on her way to commit suicide, but sharing her stories helped her to understand she has so much to look forward to.*

I think I saved someone's life by just listening and being curious!

When we are curious about our world around us,
our experiences begin to blossom like
a young flower opening her petals
to bathe in the morning sun.

What are you curious about?

What is curiosity?

Remember An Ounce of Curiosity
may just be enough.

Write here . . .

Day 23

The Humor Elixir

明月
察秋
秋毫

an ounce of . . .

Discernment

I walked into a random bar situated on a random street in some random small town on the California Coast. Four locals were sitting on their less than random stools, which were wrapped around the corner of the bar.

As I walked in, one of the men grabbed the remote control for the big screen TV and quickly changed the channel. He was not hiding the drastic action he had just taken. In fact, he was flaunting it.

"We are not watching that stupid soccer, where they roll around on the ground for no reason at all!" he exclaimed, and his three partners in crime on the corner of the bar nodded emphatically. Not only were they drunk; but they were also spot-on. I had entered the bar out of desperation hoping to find a TV and watch the second half of one of the games, being played by two of the best teams during the most recent World Cup.

I stood frozen. I was so unclear whether I should simply turn around and walk out or stand and fight. At that moment I remembered my own medicine. I asked myself, "What do I need an ounce of?"

Humor! Came the reply from deep within.

"Shots for everyone!" I screamed.

Out of nowhere, someone threw the TV remote in my direction, and all the Gentlemen who sat at the corner of the most random bar simply started laughing.

Remember laughter is always a beautiful choice.

*Don't forget to laugh as you go through
your day; it truly is so important.*

What makes you laugh?

What makes the person most important to you laugh?

Write here . . .

Day 24

An Old Adage

明月
察秋
毫

an ounce of . . .

Discernment

One of my favorite clients had quite a profound mantra, which he would share with anyone at the drop of a hat.

"I am the cool, calm, collected dude at the center of the storm!" He would almost chant on demand.

He came to me asking for help to better understand why his life was always in such turmoil.

"Would you call your life a little bit of a storm?" I asked him during our first session.

*The old adage claims,
"…be careful what you ask for."*

*I believe we should "get clear about what it is
that we ask for since we will get it."*

What is your mantra?

*Does your mantra require the equivalent
of a storm for you to shine?*

Is your mantra in need of conscious evolution?

What would be your newly evolved mantra?

Write here . . .

The
OUNCE PROJECT™

Day 25

This Too Shall Pass...

明
察
秋
毫

an ounce of . . .

Discernment

I held the question "What shall I do with my life?" in my soul and picked a tarot card that told the following story:

A king who had everything sent his Wiseman to find the ring of pure knowledge and wisdom. The Wiseman found the Shaman who held the ring, and the Shaman said, "I will give this over to the King on one condition: he does not remove the stone and read the message beneath containing ultimate wisdom until his most dire moment."

Soon after, the King's kingdom was taken, and as he ran for his life, his horse died. With his pursuers gaining and his death pending, he removed the stone from the ring and read, "This too shall pass."

Sometimes even when we are faced with our most dire moments, our most critical decisions, we may just need to pause.

Almost as if we are allowing the moment to sink in fully.

Hold your ground!

Hold your center and let the moment reveal itself to you.

What are the things that you may be trying to force into being?

Hold your ground, hold your center!

Write here . . .

Messages from Their Journeys for You . . .

Write here . . .

I know I should be looking within, but
last night I purchased a scented candle to
make our home smell more like a spa, and
it felt glorious. Today, I spent some time
decluttering the bathroom and kids room.
That, too, felt liberating, but there were also
some defeatist feelings in reaction to the
overall clutter all around. I know it will take
some time for our home to get to a minimal,
uncluttered state. I almost accept the fact that
it may NEVER get there. It's all stuff. Literally
and figuratively mountains of stuff we have
(and don't have) and the chaos surrounding
all that. But an ounce. An ounce of serenity!
When I received an ounce reminder today, I
dropped everything — all the thoughts and
to-do's and gave myself a warm foot soak for
a few minutes. It was wonderful.

AN

Write here . . .

Today is a perfect ounce because I decided to spend the day in the office as opposed to at home. I often think I get more done when I'm at home, but today has been quite the opposite. By being present with those around me, I have been infused with ideas and inspiration. I have enjoyed laughter and just everyone's general energy. It has been nice to be connected and present with my work tribe.

AH

The
OUNCE PROJECT

Write here . . .

My story has been that I cannot trust myself...
very convoluted I am realizing.... I am really
GOOD at making up stories. I need one less
ounce of imagination and Self oratory skills
for sure

WW

Write here . . .

A favorite childhood movie of mine is *Austin Powers: International Man of Mystery*. A theme of the main character is that he is embarrassed by who he is. Throughout, parts of him are brought up and made fun of, such as how he dresses, that he has bad teeth and how he uses Swedish Made Penis Enlargers. As I grew into my 20's, I started realizing how I didn't fully fit in the culture I was surrounded by in New York. Once I got to explore Europe, I noticed the NYC culture wasn't the only way people lived. It's cool to remember how much I connected to this movie, but I never realized my connection in this way, a sort of loving sympathy for a man out of place. I do stand proud now in my pursuits and interests.

TB

The OUNCE PROJECT™

Write here . . .

I ask for compassion. Understanding I
understand the Divine universe is in charge,
I pull the innocence card and remind myself
to treat others as if they are a kindergartner
on the first day of school. Compassion.

VS

The
OUNCE PROJECT™

Chapter Four

The Integration Triad

Day Twenty-Six – Day Twenty-Eight

Remember it has been a full journey to this point and so integration is a critical part of the process so please complete the final three days.

Remember just an ounce at a time.

Remember if you can master The Integration Triad, your entire life will change in magical ways.

Day 26

忠信篤敬

an ounce of . . .

Prayer

Our Father,
Who art in heaven,
Hallowed be thy name.
Thy Kingdom come.
Thy will be done,
On earth as it is in heaven.
Give us this day our daily bread;
And forgive us our trespasses,
As we forgive those who trespass against us;
And lead us not into temptation,
But deliver us from evil,
For Thine is the Kingdom
And the power
And the glory
Forever and ever.

Amen.

The Lord's Prayer

I spent 13 days in the ICU waiting room
as someone I loved lay in a coma.

The one thing I learned from the experience
of spending so much time in that room
was everyone knows how to pray.

I watched as family members and loved ones
of ICU patients prayed while in the waiting room.

Everyone knows how to pray, irrespective
of your God or your belief.

Everyone knows how to pray!

How do you pray?

What do you pray for?

When you pray, what do you hear?

Let us Pray!

Write here . . .

Day 27

知恩圖報

an ounce of . . .

Gratitude

Today I am grateful for life, as messy and as thick as it can get from time to time. I am grateful for you. Thank you!

What does an ounce of gratitude mean to you?

What are you grateful for in this moment?

*What are the things you know you should
be grateful for, yet it is just too hard
at the moment to feel gratitude?*

Write here . . .

The
OUNCE PROJECT™

Day 28

融會貫通

an ounce of . . .

Integration

I remember listening to a story featured on RadioLab about the transition of a caterpillar into a butterfly. I was blown away to discover caterpillars have wings. They have wings! Caterpillars crawl around on the ground and yet they have the capability of flying. That fact made me think about human DNA. There's so much of our DNA that scientists do not yet understand? Why it is there? Maybe that dark matter, or junk, was intentionally built into our DNA and in it, we have stored our wings. What if we only need to cocoon and evolve, like the caterpillar and the butterfly, for us to discover our built-in ability to fly?

The radio show also examined the process of transformation, tracking what happened inside the chrysalis after the caterpillar surrenders its life and takes on a new appearance as a pod. They found inside the chrysalis everything first turns to goo. Then, like the most complicated jigsaw puzzle ever created, all of the goo reforms itself into a fully functioning, unique and beautiful butterfly. It's as if all the parts of the butterfly already existed within the insect we once knew as a caterpillar, and then with nothing added except death and rebirth — WALLAI I — it becomes an entirely new version of itself, the butterfly.

I imagine tiny little workers inside the chrysalis

slaving away night and day, screaming at each other, "Where does this go? Do we need this part in this model?" Those tiny little butterfly workers innovate and craft a unique, one-of-a-kind, custom-built creature of pure perfection and beauty. Like a snowflake, so many have come before but not like this, not like this!

On the journey from goo, when do those tiny little workers inside of the chrysalis say, "Enough is enough?" How do they know when they have traveled deep enough, far enough, and melted enough into goo — pure goo — so that the rebuilding process may begin?

I once read somewhere that you should pick one book and only one book and read it over and over again. As you read the same book again and again or watch the same movie again and again, you will see things that you missed the first time through.

It will be as if the book is opening up to you sharing its innermost secrets. I believe however it is not the book that changes over time, but it is ourselves that shift, it is ourselves that open up and allow our inner wisdom to blossom.

FYI – choose your book or movie wisely!

What did you learn during today's integration as opposed to the integration process from day 14?

What does it mean for you to integrate?

How do you integrate?

Write here . . .

Messages from Their Journeys for You . . .

Write here . . .

My listening skills falter when I get scared.
Then I get frustrated because I think you can't
hear me.

TB

Write here . . .

I am bawling just now from this animated movie the kids were watching about a sick boy who was fighting for his life. I am so lucky that all my kids have had to deal with (so far) are broken bones and coughs and colds and the occasional stomach ache. I thank my lucky stars every day that BOTH my kids are healthy. That truly is priceless. Plus… even though I complain about the weariness of an office job, I do benefit from a generous health care package in case of emergencies. I also want to note the great conversation I had today. It was a fun chat about New York City life. I knew about all his references to fancy restaurants and shops in SoHo. I lived that life. I experienced that life. It wasn't just a movie or TV show. It was a life that many people dream about.

AH

The
OUNCE PROJECT

Write here . . .

I explored anger and hopelessness today. I
looked at my anger around systems, political,
legal, community, education, money, etc.
I wondered where are the system for hope,
joy, love, belonging, worthiness, acceptance
and self mastery?

TB

The
OUNCE PROJECT™

Write here . . .

I am connected to the earth, to God and to myself. My true self knows it is loved and not alone but part of a divine dance. Everything I have and am comes from God. I share this connection with all living things, and I am joyful.

RH

The
OUNCE PROJECT

Write here . . .

Yesterday when I didn't have my ounce
email I manifested my own. Pulled a card...
KNOWING and discovered that knowing has
peace alongside it as a partner... tandem...
no need to prove or interject or interrupt or
control. Just know. Just be. Good exercise
and knowledge. :) I am grateful

WW

Write here . . .

I have played so many roles to so many people:

> The villain
> The hero
> The crazy one
> The lover
> The mother
> The father

This I will no longer do. I am conscious and aware of how I influence others. And the perspective I show them. What they chose to take/see is more of a reflection of themselves. But I am always the role of love
I am of truth.
I am of presence.

NB

The
OUNCE PROJECT

Write here . . .

This morning I asked my soul what it needed an ounce of. It asked for understanding. I am pushing myself past the comfort level as my business coaches are so fired up about Success.... I just need to honor my hibernation time... it is winter after all! So I prayed that my 6:30 biz coach would have some understanding that I can not do more than I am all ready. So I shuffled the cards... and pulled the magic card.... it was UNDERSTANDING!!! A STRONG declaration that the universe hears me and the universe supports me!!!! I understand I need to live in my own pace... making new friends... remodeling the home... resting... eating good food... studying... charging my three treasures. Ahhhhhhhh life is good.

VS

The
OUNCE PROJECT

From Here to There . . .

Thank you for being brave and navigating the past 28 days into An Ounce of Discernment.

So what is next on this journey?

You have now had the opportunity to experience the process of asking yourself: *What do I need an ounce of?*

Please feel free to use this question as part of your daily practice and experience how your world blossoms ounce by ounce.

Please feel free to begin this 28-day process once again. You will find that each of these words, each of these ounces takes on their own new meaning for you. Remember you have range, and each of these words also has their own vibrational signature and their own range.

And please visit our website: TheOunceProject.com and discover additional meditations and books to help you on your path.

Many blessings to you, Dear Soul.

www.ingramcontent.com/pod-product-compliance
Lightning Source LLC
La Vergne TN
LVHW091215080426
835509LV00009B/1003